The Goddess Of The Hunt Is Not Herself

The Goddess Of The Hunt Is Not Herself

Poems by
Sam White

Slope Editions

New York | New Hampshire | Massachusetts

Published by Slope Editions

www.slopeeditions.org

Library of Congress Cataloging-in-Publication Data

White, Sam, 1973 -
    The Goddess of the Hunt is Not Herself / Sam White. — 1st ed
    p. cm.
    ISBN 0-9718219-7-6 (pbk. :alk. paper)
    I.Title.

PS3623.H5788G63 2005
811'.6--dc22
                                2004027837

Cover & Interior Design by Winsor Pop
Cover photograph by McKenzie Burrus-Granger
Layout by Jonathan Link

Printed in the United States of America

9 8 7 6 5 4 3 2 1

FIRST EDITION

for Gillian

Acknowledgments

The following poems have appeared, in one form or another, in the
following journals:

"Prairie"	*Jubilat*
"Her Body Your Body"	*Verse*
"Personal History"	*American Letters &*
	Commentary
"The Goddess of the Hunt Is Not Herself"	*Ploughshares*
"Snake Hunting at Night"	*Ploughshares*
"Loved One"	*Ploughshares;*
	Isn't it Romantic, an
	Anthology of Love Poems
	by Younger American Poets
	(Verse Press)
"God, Numero Uno"	*The Colorado Review*
"Dear Bastard"	*The Colorado Review*
"How Were You, Bird?"	*The Colorado Review*
"Gone into the Last Picture"	*Slope.org*
"Life in a Big Sweater"	*Slope.org*
"There Are Four Things Between Us"	*Slope.org*
"Method"	*Conduit*
"Specificity"	*Volt*
"Circling Flock"	*Volt*
"Creation Myth"	*Electronic Poetry Review*
"Girl with a Baboon Heart"	*Lit*
"The End of January"	*Lit*
"Milkpod"	*Crowd*
"White Crown of Our Dystopia"	*Both*
"Tuesday Night"	*The Boston Review*
"Derelict Condition"	*The Journal of Aesthetics*
	and Protest

*Thank you to all my family, teachers, and friends who helped me along
the way, especially Rob, Matthew, and Peter.*

*

*"Life in a Big Sweater," "Prairie," "Dear Bastard," "God, Numero Uno,"
"Girl with a Baboon Heart," "White Crown of Our Dystopia," "Theme,"
"Specificity," "Gone into the Last Picture," "How Are You, Bird," and
"There Are Four Things Between Us" are all dedicated to Ted Lee, Karen
Munro, Sally Keith, and to the spirit of the night they were created.*

"Milkpod" is for August Graves.

*

*The final line of "Tuesday Night" was appropriated and altered from
Frank O'Hara's "Hatred."*

Contents

Three

The Sun Brings Hope

These discolorations by visitors
whom I cannot speak words to
exceed my senses by half.

Which are you, they seem to read,
an experiment that worked,
or light lurking in silence?

Swans have left me and cry out
for further lacustrine love,
but I have left them as happenstance.

So many roundabout jackals
inhabit my sleep
that I encounter them like a hotel

of silhouettes.
Low laid the one who had me.
I have another mother?

And is she a gorgeous didact?
And does she have confetti on her shoes?

One

Life in a Big Sweater

I am going down
slowly. I am thinking
we are alone in this knit:
you and me and me and me.
I love you. Have I told you
I am hotter in this sweater.
They are building a long list
on the far side of town.
The grass works its way
to my socks. I am unshod
like an aged whisker from the lawn.
I am under you, on top.
Far off a light blinks
in the deep stretch of a window.
Part of me lives in a crow's beak.
Part of me is nest.

Circling Flock

I am often close.
Beneath the circling flock,

I am often a whirlpool
in its first revolution,

its last and twisting dot,
it's my face at the bottom of my well

irising out to a nightscape,
clouds, the sea flying,

its boundless pile,
an open boat grows, into a boy,

cupped and pitching,
the sun holds everything,

nothing. Is that breath
on my cheek absent the island?

Prairie

On the plains we saw them,
oversized beasts of intelligence
on the fringe worrying the dust.
There's a place on a woman's body.
They ran and ran as if against us. As if,
I am open to suggestions.
There's a place on a man's body.
Which opens and opens.
A place I go to, like you
on this side. They
ran and ran. A fine dust.
The lights beyond them
a string of spit.

Personal History

Here is the rope of your life's sunsets,
each pastelled thread a part
returning you to your first walk on the beach.

Here is dune grass, your mother's fingers
through your hair, the sea a fit of rabbits,
someone's hand like your hand

keeping the shape of the face
moments after the face is gone.
There's a meadow of rain in headlights,

and later vague sheep,
wool on the nail,
claw-marks of dogs.

The receivership is whole and ghosted.
The house is dark and shining
scissored out by storm.

Wing-beats of the swimming pool.
Sometimes you wake robed in the lee
and the sky flags like a bodiless shirt.

The girl's face, released
from its stem, is numerous, hovering.
Wind was the plan.

Tuesday Night

The ghost in my mouth holds me close
        to his fondness, to his waiting,
he has my eyes, my sea legs, my fractions
and interest in mind.
                I raise a little lantern

to his observance and grow a little older.
I rinse my face for launch
like victory against the blinds. But my face is returned

wherever I look. I look at the moon and my mouth
is all hooves. I can barely say what had me holding my breath.
Maybe nothing will come of this. Where now,

my little light? Forests thicken. Foot rests quicken.
        You are all in my feelings.
                        Am I closer
to the mirage rising, camels and palm fronds,
the fanning that reveals itself

            as blood built on blood. The friends I had.
I am no longer afraid of their kisses.

Dear Bastard

How are you, bastard? How much time
in the stem of that cigarette?
Is it enough? Do you crawl through
your newspaper shreds? I know your father.
I know the man who arced the myth.
I know that evening: wild ache of night growth.
The engine gurgled in our legs. The single
bird sparked from far off.
It was the drop of her hair that he remarked on,
the one time we spoke, a phone book
of sun on our shoulders,
his truck within sight.

God, Numero Uno

Black window. Hard fall
into the manure pile. Straw steaming
spoil of dark coins. I'm on my knees
hammering fence along the line.
Black window. The apple trees
waste roadside. A basketball thuds
to sullen fruit. You know, I had something,
for a while in my hands, not a word,
but a tool for the ages. I had
a shafted fork, the drop of a spade.
In this rut there were bearings. Hammer.
Hammer. The pasture breaks
to a grid. The weeds to my knees.
Black window. Black window.
Something ecstatic in the elms.
All the branches are one picture.

Girl With a Baboon Heart

She speaks as you might, stuttering
around the speck of meaning.
On the subway I am hers.
She holds something like a handbag
between her legs. Between stops
she slides a finger down its latch.
Listen, she says, these tracks,
this racket is so deeply wooden.
A cry into the inverted canopy.
I am going home now. It's nearly night,
and I must, my red ass to the moon.

Rag

A body tumbling down blocks the sun
but accentuates delicate mountain growth.
From below each swimmer radiates his urchin light.
The smallest among us are festival lovers.
The largest, rainbows. A month cycle of moons
in the runner's passing feet,
and not one of me will stop her.
I'm thirty-one follicles in a horsehair pillow.
I'm a real human living it backwards.
Cities slide closer to clouds and cloud
their assumptions. Many a friend
is shrunk to an itch. The little schoolhouse
stands itself up, hogged by fire, it knows nothing
of what's happening, it's fast
approaching the spark within its walls,
call it once in a lifetime, call it a zenith,
call it a camel that urged the first step,
a canyon, when down from the summit.
It's dusk. It's not dusk.
It's many blackened fountains.

Snake Hunting at Night

We keep this distance.
One distance.

Many of us.
From the guide

with the snake
in the pillow case.

Though no safe
distance. So we

close in.

*

He says the venom
would end it

in minutes,
an errant life

closed in,
now coiled

and digestive,
now currented

lashing at the bag,
a line snapping

on a loose jib —
the whip end

of billowing expanse.

*

In the choked brush
the flashlight is weak

for their eyes,
the swashy green

of sea water.
The idea of coming about

*

in sailing, is to make
the craft indiscernible

to the wind.
Nothing there.

Then, *oh yes,*
lucent beads.

*

The prow catches
and goes that way.

The sea water trusses
into chops.
*

The shore is a white root.

*

Many sets, in the dark,
of eyes, a contagion

of lights, as one
idea can come

to many minds at once,
in order that one

person act,
in order that

it come about,

the question present
in the mind

of the man
meeting the woman

at the gate,
he thinks and

does not say,
I remember you

differently.

Shortage

Still, it is not too late,
a flock in the sun
might be different.

Go far away,
stand on the edge
of a flower somewhere.

On the dumb street
a love
scattered its lights.

On the same street
a crouch of shadows
wishes to be.

In the beginning, this scrap
belongs to someone.

All the Trumpets

Someone must have wanted
something proclaimed

a love, a unity,
a tear in the earth

where skeins of dead souls
braid up to a cloud,

a clearing to which
all the trumpets fell

trumpeted by their own descent.

*

And though the hot air balloon

was an afterthought of farmland,
it contained our deepest wish

for agreement.
Those irregular summers

we heaved our heads into
were something together,

but ever so quietly
a friend may go.

*

These beds
have strange compartments.

I've woken in the afternoon sun
feeling perfectly make-believe.

Two

White Crown of our Dystopia

I have come into your chamber.
I have begun the process that will make me a man.
The floors have something on their mind.
They have that twinkle about them,
as if their short life
were to come to their lips.
I will be a man before you.
I will become something other
than you expected. I have tiny shoes,
which I wear when the lights grow.
I do a little dance in my corner,
which is my corner. There's more
when we finish here. There's more,
take my tiny word.

Milkpod

When I was hanging,
I had my hanging thoughts.
She crouched by the pond.
Her fingers were smaller
and fed the nibbling.
Life in a silver arc.
If I could keep her from the thirst
that grows its shell an ocean,
I could return to my dirt.
Spring and willows yellow. The day ends
in a blush. It began: be a good
guard, when I was not
a good guard.

He Often Begins His Selection by Some Half Monstrous Form

What struck me was the illustration of the act,
the sweet juices of varieties, the perfect gradations
of fossils as in sunset. The swiftest, the coexisting,
the slim, the innate, all embedded in their own instance.
Then at once, there were flowers. Seedlings
with their bulky sexes raising pyramids
from their advantage. Amazing.
A cub might be born. A volcanic island might
fire, then thickness, the giraffe once knotted
might yield a buffalo, as into each generation
the mule might vegetate or the wolf
scrabble clover.
Wind and its descendents
carry vigorous pine scent.
In summer comes broad weather,
bees over stamen. In fall the shriveled antler
experiments on insects as insects experiment on it.
Kingdoms in the unoccupied, the intercrossing,
eggs lying loose at the bottom. With winter
the trachea roots in the lung,
one or two laws through which to breathe, sleep.
A sprig unboxes a mountain. And birds, needful birds. To be
warmly colored and inheriting atmosphere. Orange foil. Yellow
string. To straggle from the accident of one's nest
and take heart.

Poem

Give me infusions
of your mountainside
and I'm your headlong
disaster humming lithe
segments of our elegy.
Incur me. Infer me.
Draw me to your proof.
You are my arms, my sleeping.

Her Body Your Body

Her body your body,
scarves in slow motion,
whole fields flap in thought,

the dam goes limp
and cries all night
through transformers to every room

and the glow from the wall
is simple, exerted,

and grass in your ears on waking,
a distance so voluptuous

you'll take it.

Sundown
and the lake shows the movie of its birth.

The little that was left
handled absently.

A buoy glides
upon waves, from chain, from trap.

Her body your body,
over and over
townships, and fire, and ash.

Lower the Dachshund into the Mountainous Panorama; It was the Missing Segment and Now Bravely Yips into the Frontier

All day I am happy; my elevated toadstool,
my less familiar koala, you drop your shadow
so elegantly I nearly forget your useful feet.
A dusk that pulls us. A beagle's nose
filibustering long into the night. You are part
argument. You are part snail's unconsciousness
lightly along the walk. I am your one good
paragraph, bendy legs, string trailing from my beak.
Our highest trembling birds leave shadows
trembling microscopically on earth, was dust,
were seeds. A distinct and defining wobble
to all the smallest things. That I may find you
in a foreign place. That you'd find me.
Here in the house I spin with my mouth,
how we travel, half brush stroke, half metric mile.
Our pre-existing oceans, how they lift the eyes
To you I come, pollen weighting my knees.
To you beneath fruit-bats never looking back.
Beautiful one, there are birds that never land
and they are weary birds. But there are altitudes
for sleep. Every closed eye magnifies
the planet. Let us fall to dream.

When She Left I Was Just Another Tree

Singing down the corridor
her mouth burned mine to coal
through two hundred sand-filled days.
TV bore its futures.
A bear extinguishing in a stream.
The me who was me showering.
While I waited for the kiss within
the lock a pretense passed. A light
between water and moon.
Moon and water. Down
on the beach pressing my hand.
The cold mass. Its reason.

The End of January

How I lumped toward you
not feeling wrong.

Derelict Condition

Such leaves as these seem bright,
social, and overindulged,
vegetating in my milieu,
my milieu which has
eaten my face, my
penis and
loves me hysterically.
O how I'm stabbed to the ground —
a feather, a nation, leaves.

Theme

Listen clowns,
you know how to do this.
Laughing is a gesture
like breaking an arm.
It's done. You know the way
the mouth splits to its simple yolk.
You know me and my hoopfuls
of tiny dogs. What do you have
beside your masterful wit?
I have a pony, and a switch.

Method

I have to be somewhere. I have to watch someone sleep and stay
until she wakes. There are enough potatoes in this room to run one
clock for a year, or remove one voice from circulation. And it would
sound like deep space. And it would sound like fuck. It's late in the
season. Take me limbless, put me limbless. Bury me without the
helium hills where they left the infants to die. Light enough to hover
above your shoulders. Swarming you for land. All the oyster shells
sobbed into a pile. All the trees topped by sun then everything split
down the center. It's a wood grain — showers over a landscape — so
every gesture is up and down: the sanding, the painting, the waving
goodbye. Will you become a flower in the dark glass or a pineapple?
At head level, the smallest window contains frozen meat. I don't know
what the largest window contains. I think it's a rock outcropping and
an ocean liner, and an ocean of two pleasures.

What Fish Brain Thought

Fish brain conjures flakes, skies
drowsy with parachutes, the beginning
of beginnings where, by particulars,
anxiety becomes openness — the first
minnow-like toe to inch
what foreign land might be. And how.
And so. There came with growth
a figuring. Fish brain thought some jazz,
a kind of wished-for-forest where
one might plot some fingers, for
everything now is fingers,
enumerating, at rest in curves,
or hotly thumbing buttons,
how like I am, fish brain thought
and thought in flakes, skies
do sleep when near me,
powdery skies of dangling legs. Not one
but many of these beginnings
looked and stopped and touched.
Please in this world.
I am not me alone.

On Migration

When all was called
to march from empty,

I went to get the paper,
wherein to lonely page numbers

my antelope had roamed,
wherein my ocean had fallen on its sword.

How far from honest food I've wandered
managing my hunger in descending bowls

and place cards so shuffled
from their tables they barely hold themselves.

Is this nowhere, the rockets
scream both bright and sad?

We couldn't wait a minute longer
for your supposed notes.

We burst into a thousand versions
of the same white star

and ended life a murmur.
I fear I'll never know

the froth as froth is taking form,
but whipped from seawater

it extends a hand
and I move to meet it

feeling it wants me
for a doctor.

Oath

I don't know about this day,
I seem to float by untouched
or papered to the corner,
lately I've slivered my oath
down to instinct I think
oath of the black fly: *cloud,*
oath of the zebra: *fence,*
that we may all push through
our pulse in the fumes,
and even so in this blur
I guess I'd like to be kissed.
But my instinct says go,
my instinct says shuffle
or shamble to grouping.
Kettled, I'm a moderate
molecule. In deadlight
I'm a sailor for feeding.

The Goddess of the Hunt is Not Herself

The goddess of the hunt
is not herself. She is tired

having waited, having sniffed around surgically.
All her arrows jiggle with nothingness,

so she turns herself inside out:

her tongue is a tail, her throat
a torso, her stomach bundled

with eyes and claws. She feels,
on her cheek, a new weather.

Angels drift by
like bodiless gowns.

Say something true
and they explode.

On every side of my mouth
there are lips. Everything above

is a tear domed on a pillow.
Everything below is an eye —

the iris a wreath of attraction —
houses woven with trees woven

with silhouettes on the beach.
Sand is the nascent memory of glass,

then all is forgotten in fire.

What forest of windows is this?
How have I seen you?

Long buried, it nuzzles the air
for a scent, for a breeze,

an opening.
Whatever happens next is your kiss.

Three

Specificity

How on this earth, this
good place, did I see
light in its crankshaft
descend to understatement.
I was younger, the last
of us. In a canoe, younger,
broader, a place of my own.

Good waste. Good curtains.
A pool in the old light. Light
drinks itself as it passes
the key. Drinks itself
as it falls in the long hands
of dusk. O specificity,
I was younger. There were
places. I had heard of them.

Goodbye Walter

My exemplar is dead,
as are my skeletal gardens,
as is my grandfather trading the delta.
My whole dead family bursts into spores.
Look at all the gum we've chewed.
Look at our canned corn.
I'll stop but I'll stop not knowing
and if you sweep your paddle through trees
I could assume anything, which alone
is reason to love you.

The new season begins with a crow
over pasture, the ongoing weapon.

If not a meadow, then we are alive.

Gone into the Last Picture

She waves and throws a ribbon to the track.
On its last tie the train shrinks to a coin.
My luggage eats at my hands. When I was young
at night the mice at night my socks
and I would wear through them.
I saw her against the window, book pages
fluttering under her chin. Sun sections
the roof in thin triangles.
A whistle and a hard crank.
You'll find the sky comes down this way,
light as a reed, machinery bared.

The Cycle of Life

To live here you must be a celebrant. You must be equal parts water and confetti. Confetti is the hand that tosses it. The heart of water is your grandmother's bucket. With buckets of heart you may eventually build a storm, then suffer exaggerations. You yourself may be exaggerated. You certainly garden. To truly garden you must be an animal. You must be covered with hair and frothing from your trowel. But real animals elude their captors. Lure your keeper into the moist straw, then disburden him of his goods. Look natural as you run. Learn the streets. Like you they're for conclusion. But the streets have hydrants. To become a hydrant you must be equal parts water and emergency. All monks are hydrants. With a wrench you may loosen a monk. Here's the cycle of life, he confesses: first you're a garden, second a fugitive garden, and lastly condensation on a window. Stare blankly through. You may eventually see a nursemaid dripping feathers and confetti. She's from the sideshow. Sideshow mountains melt into sideshow rivers hurrying to the sideshow sea. You may live by her. You may beg her to speak.

How Are You, Bird?

Should I worry? Sometimes
there's a word which escapes me,
a place against which the wind rails
and is kept out. I am warm. Shuffling
down the banister in my cashmere
and pantaloons. I think you are dead to the night.
To its overtures, to its slippage.
Do you know me yet? I have bet everything
on you, steady in your branch, a memory to yourself.

Identification

Overhead we are nothing
but clouds touching our own dials,
breathing sugar and Latin music,
thundering into each transformation

or now and then tearing our ears off,

as if our iterations cost us life.
Suppose they did and we again
in open fields of mud and rain
and we again exposed.

On Perseverance

Here within the clatter
I stop and set my books and guess
some days that nothing else will be.

Where once I envisioned iridescence
and airships and iridairships
now I sit and stare.

To what end do my windows
see themselves in other windows,
and of those found in neighbors' windows

who am I living there?
Stay within a manner of purpose.
Stay when weeks grow hair.

Hold my books and guess and
breathe a little rumor.

There are Four Things Between Us

Should I say you're one of them?
Should I say there's a place where
your hip starts and your legs end?
I think I saw you by the gas pumps.
Correct me. I think I saw you leaning
over the towel-faced kid in the dungarees.
You have something you need to say, I can tell
from the early forecast of your brows.
I saw you once over the punch bowl
making eyes at the cubes. I saw you once
a face full of fumes. I am not that much
a man. I am one name you've tossed out
speaking loosely in your sleep.

Announcement

So much goes horribly unsaid.
I wanted only a return to inquiry
where, in my arms your head
was a dreamy scallop.

But now I'm alone on a bus
and heretofore may only conjure sand,
though I sense the outer of outbuildings
and jackrabbits and others nearly freed.

How this must feel. Westward runs
the wind, the bus, the cardboard ocean,
          in beautiful heretofore,
                    in beautiful sand.

Creation Myth

Lonely continents, how far we've spun
from our million year kiss,

our million year shrug,
forever wishing back

the rotational penumbra unveiling
the latest grass, purple clouds,

carryalls overfull spilling,
everything spilling. It's sunrise

on tomorrowland. Rub all advents
from your eyes, for we begin again,

walking now upright and far
from our leathery births,

as islands spasm, volcanoes
sprinkle down boulders,

forests laugh up leaf
cutter ants. A dizzy wild.

In one short day the finch
is swapped for an owl,

the owl for a ghost.
I am half your brain

warbles the ghost.
The shadow is always touching us,

moving us around,
and how we move within it,

believing the sea
above the sea above the sea.

Black Window

I'm dumb to say what divides my agreement through the night
or how in the morning my mix of sensations agree
on one likeness smoldering, where hours after rain
the record plays to grass, luck decoded hurls down
as light on a river scattering its wealth
so it may creep uninspected, that it is finally,
huddling flourished, and at one length
winding ahead through all cancellation to cameras,
in their swim, aching, shimmering, as your waters
upon enlargement must, and I to have you with me.

Loved One

You were not gone
but asleep through the slide show,

and you were gone
the projector pointing skyward

the ceiling quivering
with our faces.

Are there many sizes of infinity?
These are stars, this the black

tank, circular glass,
a worldless plankton,

which are *leave*,
a worldless plankton,

which are *come*.
Wake now. O mountains

O upside down mountains of light.
A brick sings like a robin.

A brick screeches like a jay.
A waltz interred by the wind.

Something moves with me,
the bonfires draw back

their ever smaller
curtains of smoke.

There *are* many sizes of infinity
and only one will do,

the one that moans a little
as I slide the slipper on.

There were mists.
A waterfall fainted

across my shoulders.
Many houses

in the valley at night
and yours was where

I stopped.